Odds & Ends

Chelsea Fry Parker

Presentation by *BookLeaf Publishing*

Web: www.bookleafpub.com

E-mail: info@bookleafpub.com

ISBN: 9789357441063

First edition 2023

DEDICATION

To my mom,

someone who never gave up on me.

To my sibling,

someone who always gives it to me straight.

To my husband,

someone who puts up with me no matter what.

PREFACE

This started out as a spontaneous decision that I started doubting almost immediately. It then quickly turned into a project that helped me reconnect with my creativity. Prior to starting this project, I hadn't had much success writing anything for quite a spell. So there is a bit of chaos in how these poems were written as I struggled to find inspiration. Ultimately, I decided to leave everything in the order they were written, with the exception of "Writer's Block," because I liked the organic feel.

"Writer's Block" wasn't originally going to be included because it started as a joke when I was extremely frustrated. Since it was originally not intended to see the light of day, it is an unfiltered example of my sense of humor. It ended up turning out quite well, so I decided to include my snarky frustration.

So please enjoy the product of my caffeine-fueled fervor!

A Simple Delight

A cup of tea, a simple delight
This sip starts my day with meditation
The fresh water flows and the kettle boils
Tea leaves unfurl and float gently through it
Steam dances up before disappearing
Here in this moment, I sit with myself
This moment of calm, this moment of peace

There is a lot to be done now today
It can all wait while I collect myself
For right now, it is just me and my tea
This meditative calm, quiet, and peace
When it is all gone, I will start my day
Even so, this I do only for me
A cup of tea, a simple delight

Not Today

Nope, not today.
I'll try again tomorrow.
I don't care what they say!
I'll stay right here,
Where I'm cozy and warm,
With my cats sleeping near.
I think that it's best,
Since my head is a mess,
To stay here and rest.

Raindrop

Raindrop falling quietly from above
Above the clouds are dark as ink
Ink sky as the hidden sun sets for night
Night rain quiets the world, enveloping it in a dream
Dream now my friend, now rest
Rest, enjoy this evening overture
Overture of wind rustling, water falling, peacefulpresence
Presence here in this moment, quiet like a raindrop

Sneasel

Sometimes, I stare into the void.
Usually the void stares back,
From a dark room or blanket.
And usually the void wants a snack.
Our void has many options, mostly about food,
Of which he thinks there's a lack.
Such is our life
With a cat that is black.

Conversation with Loki

Why are you yelling at me?
I literally just got home.
Yes, I can see you feel strongly about it.
Did that really all happen today?
I think you're exaggerating.
Okay, fine, it really is that bad.
Oh my goodness!
No! Get off that!
Why are you like this?

For My Husband

Here's another sappy poem for you
I love you, I do
Even with your bad puns
Or when I trip on your shoe

I'll be there for you
Really, it's true
Even when things get hard
When you are sick of life or with the flu

We'll celebrate together
When there's fair weather
Or just getting through the week
For success in any endeavor

So long story short
I'll be your support
You're stuck with me now
You're partner in crime, you're cohort

(Dedicated to Dalton)

Winter

Grey is the cloud,
A blanket stretched out above.

White is the snowflake,
Skittering in the wind.

Brown is the tea,
Warming my soul.

Yellow is the fire,
Burning warm and bright.

Cold is the winter.
Warm is this house.

Christmas

T'was the week before Christmas
And we'd all lost our minds.
Our plans and our patience,
Like a yarn ball unwinds.

The presents are wrapped,
Stacked under the tree.
Most of them anyway,
We're still missing three.

One went to Canada.
We're not really sure why.
One is three streets over,
I note with a sigh.

The other is here,
But I've run out of tape.
And if I go to the store,
I may never escape.

So here we sit,
All the chaos in sight.
Merry Christmas y'all
And to y'all a good night!

Rainbow of Office Supplies

Red Swingline stapler, snapity snap.
Orange eraser I found in a drawer.
Yellow highlighter that's almost dry.
Green sticky notes, probably need more.
Blue pens, we buy by the gross.
Indigo pens, lose them and you're done for.
Violet mug, my funny little owl.
A rainbow of supplies all in my drawer.

Winter Grey

Winter is seen as cold and grey,
Seemingly the same from day to day.
But variations abound
With subtleties on display.

In clouds, what shades can be found?
Shadows of charcoal and iron astound.
The dove grey cloudscape
With highlights of silver is wound.

Graphite streets wear snow as capes
And platinum frost starts to take shape.
The goose down puff of your breath in the air
As all heats seems to escape.

Though things are cold and bare,
Beauty can be seen if you're aware.
Underappreciated though it may be,
Grayscale can have its own flair.

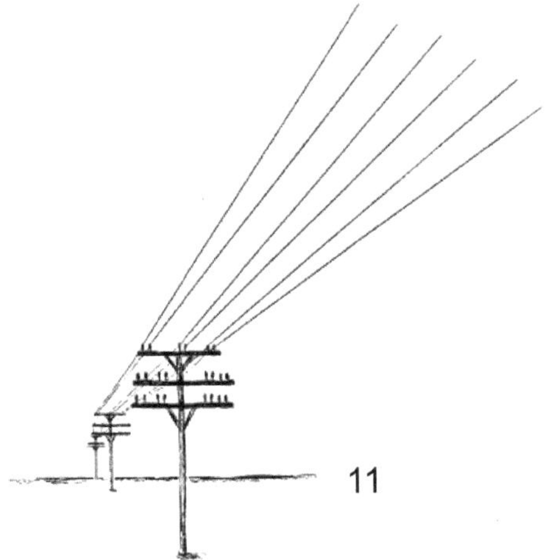

Rainy Day

Drip
Drip
Drop

Rain slips
Falling from a leaf
Landing with a plop

Pitter patter
Pitter patter

Falling in the roof
Land and then splatter

Splish
Splash
Splish

Puddles form
Then a car rolls by
And they're gone with a swish

Frost

Frost forming
In a frigid frame
Fascinating frozen fractals

A frozen film
Fracturing and filtering
The faint first light

Festooning the fanlight
With a frigid fresco
Faint but effervescent

Candlelight

I turn the lights low
The day has simply been too much
With a flicker
I bring a candle to life

As I take this moment
And breathe deeply
I let the quiet wash over me
With the occasional crackle

The dusky light flutters
A welcome break
Away from the stark and bright
Letting my eyes rest

This is how I'll end my day
No responsibilities
Even if just temporarily
In calming candlelight

Spring

A whisper of warmth
Breaks the cold
Like dawn
Ending the night

Slowly, gradually
The world stirs again
Starting soft and small
Animals begin to call

Winter cold begins to thaw
As the first warmth of Spring
Creeps across the fading snow
Coaxing life back from slumber

The whispers will become
A diverse symphony, in time
But for now, the musicians tune
And we wait with bated breath

Forest Witch

I want to live
In a mushroom house
Surrounded by magical animals
Like cleaning doves and a sewing mouse

Outside, maybe some gnomes
And fairies flitting about
Fantastically colored toadstools
And a wolf I'd call Scout

With my critter friends
I'd pick herbs in the woods
Sometimes I'd go to town
To sell my crafts and goods

When I got home
I'd have some tea
And think about taking a trip
Maybe to the mountains or sea

It would be a simple life
Just enjoying each day
Making different things
And seeing what creatures come to play

Moon Phases

Quiet sky
The new moon rises
The world waits

A stirring
Waxing, gaining light
Brightening

Night descends
The full moon rises
Dancing bright

In pale light
This world comes alive
Giddy souls

Hide again
As silver light wanes
Growing gloom

Quiet sky
The new moon rises
The world waits

Summer

Clear and warm
The days are bright
The summer breeze
Carrying the day by
It stirs the leaves
And cicada song

Kids run barefoot
Fresh grass
And rich earth
Tickling their toes
New discoveries
Are everywhere

As night descends
Rain scents the air
Thunder rumbles
Far away
To wash away
The dusty haze

No threat is here
Just renewing rain
Cooling the air
Refreshing the trees
Bringing new life
And a bright new day

Fall

As the leaves fall,
The air is rich
With loam and earth.
Yet, still crisp
As the chill creeps in.
For now though,
The world is still bright and soft.
With pumpkins and sweaters,
Bright laughter
And warm drinks.
A tapestry of life
Before winter hibernation.
Rich reds:
Currant, crimson, and scarlet.
Lavish oranges:
Squash, cider, and marmalade.
Plentiful yellows:
Gold, corn, and honey.
Hinted browns:
Coffee, cedar, and walnut.
Such a luscious display!
Bringing a smile to the soul.
Breathe it all in!
This natural festival
To carry us through the winter.
Enjoy the celebration!

Ode to Cheese Curds

Cheese curds are tasty!
Helping satisfy the munchies,
Especially in the afternoons.
Exquisite fried goodness!
Sometimes they can be a side,
Even a meal on their own.
Cheese curds are the best snack!
Unparalleled in their pop-ability.
Rich and warm in my belly,
Dunked in sauce or plain.
Snacks are the best!

(Dedicated to Tavi)

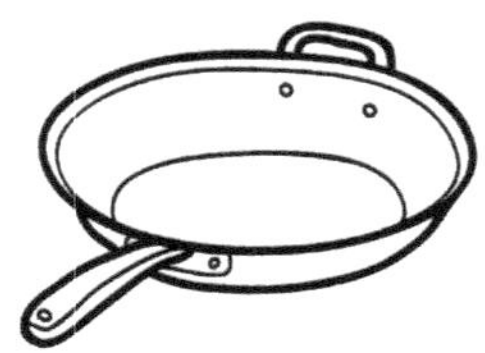

Evening Tea

A love
An obsession
A mug
Some leaves
The water clear
And boiled fresh
Another cup
But to end my day
Another deep breath
No caffeine
Just relaxing herbs
Thank you all
And good night

Writer's Block

Write poetry, I said.
It'll be fun, I said.
I've had luck
Writing it in the past.
I have so many ideas,
Rattling around in my head!
I grab my pen to write
And poof!
Suddenly my mind is blank.
I can't count syllables...
Or think of rhymes...
Or spell...
This is fine.
Totally fine.

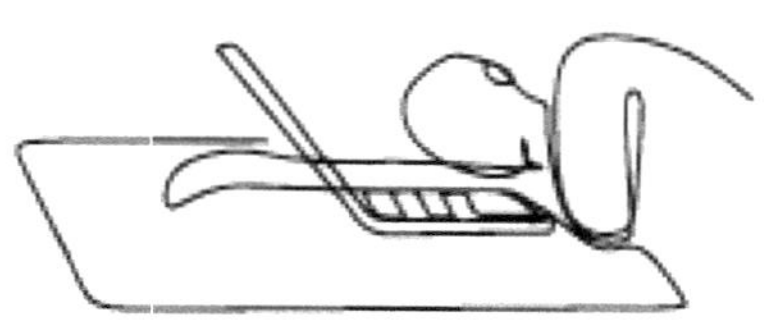

Printed in the USA
CPSIA information can be obtained
at www.ICGtesting.com
LVHW020701311223
767624LV00084B/3223